ideals®
CHRISTMAS

*May these be your gifts at Christmas:
warm hearts and shining faces
surrounding you to make your home
the happiest of places.*

—AUTHOR UNKNOWN

NASHVILLE, TENNESSEE

Colors of Christmas

Nora M. Bozeman

Reds and yellows, blues
   and greens—
Christmas paints her
   Yuletide scenes.
Brilliant cards in colors bold,
ornaments of red and gold,

festive stores and scenery,
frosty panes in filigree,
trees ashine in silvered snow,
star-strung avenues aglow,

winter white and cheeks of red,
sapphire skies hung overhead,
hanging swags of evergreens
color all my Christmas scenes.

The Lights of Christmas

Polly Prindle Katzenberger

I love the lights of Christmas,
the candle-flame that gleams
from clear unshaded windows
in golden-threaded streams.

I love each bulb that glistens
on every fragrant tree,
and every star seems brighter
at Christmastime to me.

But the little lamps that thrill me
from earth up to the skies,
are the little lights of Christmas
that shine in children's eyes.

Little Lights

J. Harold Gwynne

Somehow the little colored lights
are brighter than the rest;
of all the lovely Christmas sights,
the little lights are best.

The rows and strings of lights we see
are mirrored on the snow;
but little lights upon the trees
shine forth with mystic glow.

They shine like jewels rich and rare,
in red and blue and green;
they look like flowers, bright and fair,
that summer days have seen.

Perhaps the little lights are blessed
with healing, light and mild,
because they burn and shine their best
for Mary's little Child.

Christmas in the Country

Lansing Christman

Each of my Christmastimes through the years has been a country Christmas spent with the outdoor world around me. Each glorious Christmas offers its quiet stillness, its birdsongs, its sparkling stars, its glowing moon, its boughs brushing in the wind. I have always kept Christmas as rural and old-fashioned as possible, and nature has never failed to fulfill my dreams for a perfect holiday.

I treasure the tradition of a country Christmas. There is joy and cheer to be found in tramping the woods and winter hills, the songs coming from the chickadees and tree sparrows in the hemlocks and brushy thickets, the voices of goldfinches calling in sweeping unison from the old weed fields.

A country Christmas is a colorful one. My family has always had an indoor Christmas tree, but we also enjoy the greenery offered by the dooryard spruce and, out in the woods, the pine and hemlock. These greens are joined by reds: the berries of the dogwoods and the alders in the swamp. Snow might follow snow to blanket the hills, grass, stone, and earth, but the greens and reds still peek through the white.

Each country Christmas brings cheer and comfort and peace. The golden sun of day gives way to the glittering glory of star-filled nights. Sometimes the holiday brings snow, but cheer abounds whether or not the landscape is white. I am most at peace with an old-fashioned Christmas in the country.

Shimanek Bridge near Scio, Oregon. Image © Dennis Frates Photography.

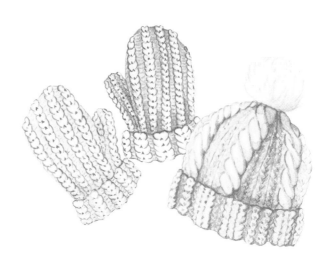

First Snow

Ruth H. Underhill

See the happy faces,
hear the sounds of cheer
made by children playing
in the first snow of the year.

See the snowballs flying;
hear the shouts of glee,
the rolling, tumbling in the snow,
as jolly as can be.

Now I see a snowman
built about halfway;
snowballs must be rolled so fast
to finish him today.

Some are sliding down the hill
as fast as sleds will go;
others make snow angels
while lying in the snow.

My, such joyful sights to see,
what pleasant sounds to hear,
made by children playing
in the first snow of the year!

Angels in the Snow

Claire Dutton Williams

What a joy it is remembering
a Christmas long ago,
lying down and making shapes
of angels in the snow.

Each child would choose so carefully
his very special place,
then, falling backwards, rapidly
create his angel lace.
Sometimes we'd make a choir
of angels, big and small,
lined up in frozen wonder;
the sight would thrill us all.

When the angels all were finished
by my playmates and by me,
they were lovelier than any
upon a Christmas tree.

Christmas Photographs

Melinda Rumbaugh

My family's Christmas traditions are well-documented. I love looking at the snapshots of my siblings and me sitting in front of the tree, surrounded by wrapping paper and laughing at kittens chasing ribbons. We have shoeboxes full of Polaroids from Christmases past—elated kids holding this doll, then that Lego set, and finally, the long-wished-for video-game console (the gift to beat all gifts and to unify the siblings in collective pleading).

We have photographs that record our traditions, but photographs themselves were also a tradition in my family. Each year after dinner at my grandmother's house, before opening gifts, we stood for the annual Christmas photos.

The ritual began with Grandmother calling out our names to report for our photos. I patiently waited my turn as she consulted the previous year's photos framed on the wall behind us. It was important to her that we repeat each photograph with precision, down to our positions in the photos. The first group was always Grandmother's children—my mom and her two brothers. Then their spouses, the in-laws (or "the outlaws," as we called them) stood together. Each family's kids then gathered: my sister, brother, and I in one photo; my cousins in another. Finally, Grandmother joined the photos, proudly flanked by all six of her grandkids.

Wearing the new clothes that we'd unwrapped just that morning, we presented ourselves before the heavy wooden front door—our backdrop—and grinned. Urged to crowd together, we moved closer, comparing height, poking each other, and cracking jokes between shots. (In that era of film cameras, the adults discouraged antics like bunny ears or funny faces, but that didn't always stop us from trying.)

Strict adherence to this tradition has given us a very clear record of the passage of time. Today, I love revisiting the photos and making note of the changes from year to year: growth spurts and hairstyles and the evolving, ill-advised fashions of the times. It's a trip down memory lane—hilarious and endearing and bittersweet.

In the early years, my siblings and cousins and I were dressed in reindeer sweatshirts with beaming, gap-tooth grins. I can see the anticipation in our faces. We couldn't wait to open our presents. The photos from our awkward preteen and teenage years featured big hair and braces—and embarrassed smiles that, if you look hard enough, were an admission that we still liked Christmas and even (gasp!) *wanted* to be with our families that day.

Boyfriends and girlfriends soon joined the mix, and then husbands and wives. Finally, one year, we added a new photograph to the shot list:

Image © Masterfile Royalty Free

a stuffed monkey, crocheted by our great-aunt Saralee, in his place. The monkey became Keith's stand-in for a couple of years, and then it stood in for others when they couldn't make it. It was important to us that everyone be accounted for in the photos.

These photographs are gold to me, the best Christmas gift Grandmother could have given us. They are a priceless reminder that family is vital and that we are linked, year after year, to one another. There in those photos, in that house on Christmas Day, we knew our places—we knew we belonged. We were Grandmother's grandkids, and she wanted a lasting record of who we were and who we were becoming.

As I look through Grandmother's photo albums, these Christmas photographs will always remind me of the things that have changed: how we've grown and aged, how far we've come as individuals, and how we miss those we've lost, including the grandmother who brought us all together and loved us so unfailingly. But the photos also show what has not changed: that we are family and, whatever comes, the love that knit us together in those photographs will never fade.

my cousin's infant daughter in a photograph with her great-grandmother. That Christmas felt special, and so full of joy.

Some years were hard. When my cousin Keith was absent because he was in the Air Force, we all worried about where he might be and what dangers he might be facing. We missed him. We held up

The Carolers

Georgia B. Adams

In the glow of the lamplight,
the carolers sing;
what a warm Yuletide spirit
their glad voices bring!

"Silent Night" softly echoes
from hearts young and old
as the story of Jesus
through music is told.

See them snuggled in mufflers
with faces aglow,
silhouetted so neatly
against driven snow!

O'er our threshold we bid them—
"Oh, do come inside
for a cup of hot cocoa
this glad Christmastide!"

Christmas Carols

LaVerne P. Larson

Lovely Christmas carols
floating on the winter air
are filled with hope and faith
for mankind everywhere.

They tell the Christmas
    stories,
old, and yet so dear,
and bring His loving message
to spread a special cheer.

How sweet the voices sound,
like angels from above,
reassuring every heart
of His great and tender love.

When the carols echo forth,
peace and joy abide;
it's good to have these
    melodies
to sing at Christmastide.

No Room

Tracy Crump

Take these verses home and have your mother help you memorize them." My first-grade teacher laid a sheet of paper on my desk.

As Mrs. Heartsfield moved on to the next student, I picked up the page and tried to decipher the unfamiliar words. I had learned a great deal in my three months of school. I could read important things like "Run, Spot, run!" and "See Jane go." But the words on this page were much longer and harder to understand.

When Mama met me outside the school that afternoon, I excitedly waved the paper at her. "I have to learn these words so I can say them in the school play."

"Let's see." She caught the flapping sheet and read a few sentences. "This is the Nativity story. Your school's first-grade classes do this each year."

"The Nativity story?" I asked.

We walked the half-block home, and as the chill December wind whipped our hair, Mama explained that the Nativity story came from the Bible and told of Jesus' birth. "You have a very important part," she said, smiling down at me.

I worked hard to learn the verses over the next two weeks. Mama helped me practice the long words every afternoon. Finally, the big day arrived.

Dressed in my best plaid skirt and a new red sweater, I stood in the wings waiting for my turn. I pulled up my knee socks as I moved closer to the front of the line where Mrs. Heartsfield directed children onto the stage. Before I knew it, I was next. Mrs. Striker, the other first-grade teacher, hovered just behind the edge of the curtain on the other side of the stage, prompting those who forgot their lines.

"All right, Tracy, it's your turn." Mrs. Heartsfield gave me a little push.

My shiny patent leather shoes tapped a staccato beat as I walked across the stage to the microphone. I stood beside two of my classmates who, dressed as Joseph and Mary, knelt beside a humble manger. Trembling, I found Mama's smiling face among the sea of parents in the auditorium, took a deep breath, and began. The words tumbled out just as I had practiced.

"And so it was, that while they were there, the days were accomplished that she should be delivered. And she brought forth her firstborn son, and wrapped him in swaddling clothes, and laid him in a manger; because there was no room for them in the . . ."

I paused. *Garage* was the word that came to mind, but somehow that didn't seem right.

Mrs. Striker saw my hesitation. "Inn!" she whispered.

"Inn!" I practically shouted. Then I turned and walked off the stage to thunderous applause.

The audience never knew how close I came to messing up one of the best-known verses in the Bible!

When I told Mama, I thought she would be frustrated after all the hours she'd put into coaching me on my part. Instead, she wrapped me in a big hug. "You did a wonderful job and pronounced the words so clearly—especially the last one!"

Another Christmas Play

Pamela Love

One third of the three kings
has almost dropped his "gold."
A cow and donkey on the stage
have whispered that they're cold.

A shepherd just forgot his lines,
and Joseph's robe's too long—
he almost tripped upon the hem
while Mary sang her song.

Then "Christ is born!" the
        angels said—
too early, it was true,
but all who heard it
        smiled once more
at the story, old and new.

Christmas

Patricia Emme

As songs of Christmas fill the air,
and Christmas magic's everywhere,
may all your loved ones far and near
be blessed with Christmas
        love and cheer.

Planting Hope

Joan Donaldson

As a young couple, my husband, John, and I lived in a small timber-framed house, in which one large room made up the entire first floor. So instead of a Christmas tree, we hung pine branches on the center beam, wrapped the boughs with colored lights, and decorated them with homemade ornaments—a red felt cardinal, wooden angels, and tin stars. We even strung lights along the roof of our animal barn so our goats could feel festive too!

The year we adopted our two sons from a Colombian orphanage, however, John and I saw a problem with our tradition. Not only could our boys not reach the overhead beam to help decorate, but the height also denied them the pleasure of smelling and touching a pine tree. And yet, now that our big room was lined with baskets of toys and more furniture, there was even less space for a Christmas tree.

"Unless we found a child-size tree," I suggested.

On the third Sunday of Advent, we loaded our sons into John's green pickup and rattled around the farm, scanning the edges of the woods. Finally, we spied a three-foot-tall white pine. We dug up the tree, plopped it into a large flowerpot, and set it beside our upright piano.

The white pine's soft needles perfumed the room and didn't prick our preschoolers' fingers. With a little assistance, the boys hung small, glittering red, gold, and blue balls. They wrapped golden tinsel and twinkling lights over the branches. John and I still decorated the overhead beam, a perfect place for the more fragile ornaments. For the next ten days, the boys reveled in their tree, hiding toys among the presents or staring at the twinkling lights. When New Year's Eve arrived, we took down our decorations.

"What should we do with the tree?" John asked. "If we set it on the porch, its roots will freeze."

"The ground hasn't frozen yet," I realized. "Let's plant it. A sign of hope for a blessed New Year."

A new family tradition took root that year, as the four of us chose a special location and transplanted the tree. Over the years, we added more trees, creating a small forest that reminded us of our family Christmases. Eventually, our sons left home for college and careers. We abandoned our family tradition and returned to decorating the beam.

A few years ago, John and I built a Victorian style home complete with a high-ceilinged parlor. But every Christmas season raced by us as we mailed off boxes and attended holiday gatherings. We strung a few lights around the porch roof and decorated the mantel with pine branches and holly, but we never got around to hauling in a Christmas tree.

Because our eldest son served in the military, he and his family traveled from one base to another, always too far away to celebrate Christmas on the farm. After a tragedy took our son's life, his widow moved with her young daughters to a city just a few hours away. This year, our three granddaughters could spend Christmas with us. A large tree would fit into the parlor, but memories of past holidays nudged that idea away.

"Let's go find a tree," I said.

In our blue pickup, we rumbled to where a three-foot-tall Douglas fir grew, just the right size to fit into a large flowerpot. Snug in our parlor, the feathery branches decorated and lit, the fir charmed the girls as we explained how the family tradition had begun. And once again, on New Year's Day, we planted our tree, remembering past joys and looking forward with hope.

Image © Melanie Defazio/Stocksy

Bits & Pieces

God gave us Christmas to give
us hope and peace in our hearts.
—*Catherine Pulsifer*

A gift, however small,
speaks its own language.
And when it tells of the love
of the giver, it is truly blessed.
—*Norman Vincent Peale*

May you have the gladness of Christmas, which is hope; the spirit of Christmas, which is peace; the heart of Christmas, which is love.

—Ada V. Hendricks

"And his name will be the hope of all the world."

—Matthew 12:21 (NLT)

Christmas is doing a little something extra for someone.

—Charles Schulz

Blessed is the season which engages the whole world in a conspiracy of love!

—Hamilton Wright Mabie

What is Christmas? It is tenderness for the past, courage for the present, hope for the future. It is a fervent wish that every cup may overflow with blessings rich and eternal, and that every path may lead to peace.

—Agnes M. Pharo

I love the excitement, the childlike spirit of innocence, and just about everything that goes along with Christmas.

—Hillary Scott

The Miracle of Christmas

Vincent Godfrey Burns

The miracle of Christmas
is a wreath upon the door;
a Christmas tree in splendor
with gifts spread on the floor;
a warm and glowing fire
in a cozy fireplace;
and happy, cheerful people
with a smile on every face.

The miracle of Christmas
is a star-filled winter night
with window after window
aglow with candlelight;

with patterns of purple shadows
along the gleaming snow;
with happy youthful voices
singing carols as they go.

The miracle of Christmas
is a Babe of long ago
and a gentle mother kneeling
by a manger crude and low;
and one star of glory shining
in the heavens up above
for the One who is the symbol
of God's everlasting love.

Keeping Christmas

Minnie Klemme

Let the star shine in your window;
let the Christ come through your door;
and the hopes and joys of Christmas
will be yours forevermore.

As it shone for seer and shepherd,
so the star still shines for you,
in its bright and ancient splendor,
keeping Christmas ever new.

To keep Christmas—here's the secret,
which I gladly shall impart—
keep the starlight in your window
and the Christ Child in your heart.

Secrets

LaVerne P. Larson

Secrets are a lot of fun
at any time of year,
but the ones that seem the best of all
are those with Christmas cheer.

They cast a special magic
and weave such pure delight
that hearts of everyone concerned
can't wait till Christmas night.

Each secret first is hidden
in a closet or a drawer,

then later wrapped with tinseled bows
to make the spirits soar.

Somehow the secret finds its way
beneath the Christmas tree,
and soon is opened up with haste
'mid shouts of hearty glee.

How good to have these secrets,
which add a glowing touch
to special plans at Christmas
for folks we love so much.

I Dream of Childhood Christmas

Bob Rowe

I dream of childhood Christmas
so many years ago,
when we were all together
and the world was white with snow.

I can see my grandma smiling
as she baked the pumpkin pie,

my mother wrapping presents,
and a gleam in each child's eye.

I can close my eyes and hear the sounds
of carols from above,
when homes were filled with laughter
and hearts were filled with love.

No Peeking!

Kristi West Breeden

In the days before the Internet and Black Friday sales, we kids waited patiently for the department store's annual Christmas toy catalog. When it arrived, Mom would ask us to go through the pages and mark what we wanted for Christmas. I took this project very seriously.

I knew better than to circle every single toy that caught my eye, so I took my time poring over the catalog and picked only the toys I *really* wanted. Then I returned the catalog to Mom and waited. Mom would say, "Don't ask questions at Christmastime." We were also taught not to sneak around, look in closets or under beds, or to shake wrapped packages. No peeking allowed!

One year, I saw a special toy in the catalog. Although it looked like a typical fashion doll with a gorgeous tan and long, flowing hair, it was nearly two feet tall! And the best part was when you twisted the top of her head, her long hair would change from blonde to brunette. As a kid, I loved playing with hair—combing, brushing, styling—so this doll was exactly what I wanted. I circled the doll advertisement and hoped for the best.

Just before Christmas, my mom and I went into the department store at the mall. As we got closer to the catalog delivery counter, Mom told me to wait while she went to pick up a package. The anticipation and secrets were more than I could handle. When Mom's package was brought out, I took a quick peek. It was the doll I wanted! I pretended I hadn't seen anything, but after the initial excitement went away, I began to feel a twinge of regret.

With Christmas just days away, I kept my secret well. When it was time to open gifts, I saw the large box wrapped in pretty Christmas paper and knew what was in it. I looked at my parents. I could see the expectation in their eyes. Wanting to please them, I carefully opened the box and put on my best surprised look. It worked. Everyone was delighted that I liked my gift.

As an adult, I've come to realize that some people like to sneak a peek at their Christmas gifts. For them, it's all part of the fun. I'm firmly in the camp that likes to wait for the surprise. When I give a gift, I like anticipating the reveal that's followed by a smile or hug, words of gratitude, or a squeal of delight. Maybe it's my mom's influence or the fact that I'm now the gift-giver, but I like preserving that moment of surprise around the Christmas tree. No peeking for me!

Family Recipes

Hash Brown Casserole

1 cup butter, divided, melted
1 10¾-ounce can cream of
    mushroom soup
1 cup sour cream

1 30-ounce package frozen shredded
    hash browns, thawed
2 cups shredded Cheddar cheese
2 to 3 cups corn flakes, crushed

Preheat oven to 350°F. In a large mixing bowl, mix ½ cup melted butter, cream of mushroom soup, and sour cream. Add hash browns and shredded cheese and mix well.

Turn into a greased 9 x 13-inch pan. Evenly spread corn flakes over mixture. Pour remaining butter over top of casserole. Bake 1 hour; serve warm. Makes 12 to 15 servings.

Brunch Fruit Salad

1 20-ounce can pineapple chunks
2 large, firm bananas, cut into
    ¼-inch slices
1 cup grapes, halved
1 15-ounce can mandarin oranges,
    drained

1 medium red apple, cubed
1 medium green apple, cubed
½ cup granulated sugar
2 tablespoons cornstarch
⅓ cup orange juice
1 tablespoon lemon juice

Drain pineapple, reserving juice. In a large bowl, combine pineapple, bananas, grapes, oranges, and apples; set aside. In a small saucepan, combine sugar and cornstarch. Add orange juice, lemon juice, and reserved pineapple juice; stir until smooth. Bring to a boil.

Reduce heat and simmer for 2 minutes, stirring often. Remove from heat; cool 5 minutes. Pour syrup over fruit to taste and gently mix together. Cover and refrigerate until ready to serve. Makes 10 servings.

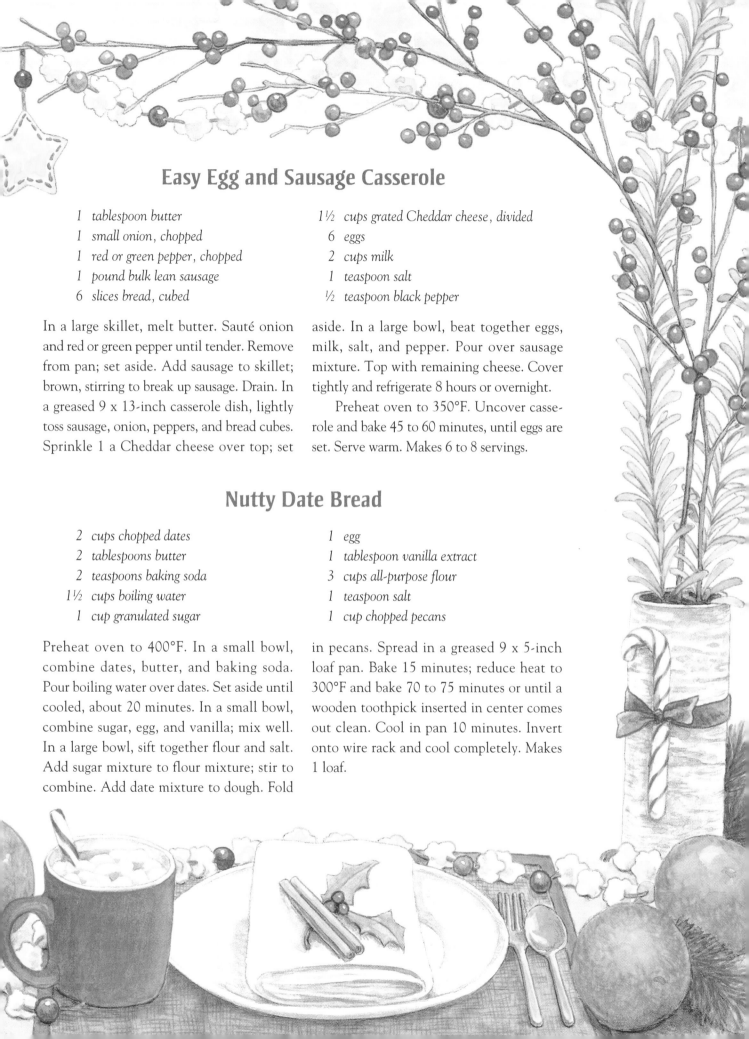

Easy Egg and Sausage Casserole

1   tablespoon butter
1   small onion, chopped
1   red or green pepper, chopped
1   pound bulk lean sausage
6   slices bread, cubed

1½   cups grated Cheddar cheese, divided
6   eggs
2   cups milk
1   teaspoon salt
½   teaspoon black pepper

In a large skillet, melt butter. Sauté onion and red or green pepper until tender. Remove from pan; set aside. Add sausage to skillet; brown, stirring to break up sausage. Drain. In a greased 9 x 13-inch casserole dish, lightly toss sausage, onion, peppers, and bread cubes. Sprinkle 1 a Cheddar cheese over top; set aside. In a large bowl, beat together eggs, milk, salt, and pepper. Pour over sausage mixture. Top with remaining cheese. Cover tightly and refrigerate 8 hours or overnight.

Preheat oven to 350°F. Uncover casserole and bake 45 to 60 minutes, until eggs are set. Serve warm. Makes 6 to 8 servings.

Nutty Date Bread

2   cups chopped dates
2   tablespoons butter
2   teaspoons baking soda
1½   cups boiling water
1   cup granulated sugar

1   egg
1   tablespoon vanilla extract
3   cups all-purpose flour
1   teaspoon salt
1   cup chopped pecans

Preheat oven to 400°F. In a small bowl, combine dates, butter, and baking soda. Pour boiling water over dates. Set aside until cooled, about 20 minutes. In a small bowl, combine sugar, egg, and vanilla; mix well. In a large bowl, sift together flour and salt. Add sugar mixture to flour mixture; stir to combine. Add date mixture to dough. Fold in pecans. Spread in a greased 9 x 5-inch loaf pan. Bake 15 minutes; reduce heat to 300°F and bake 70 to 75 minutes or until a wooden toothpick inserted in center comes out clean. Cool in pan 10 minutes. Invert onto wire rack and cool completely. Makes 1 loaf.

Christmas and Peanut Brittle

Anne Kennedy Brady

My grandma's peanut brittle is legendary. Hefty yet flaky and never sticky, it practically melts in your mouth. But it is not simple. It requires patience and gloves and a slab of marble and a friend. Gram used to make it almost every Christmas, enlisting our eager help whenever possible. But since she passed away, we simply hadn't reinstated the tradition. Until last year.

Several Christmases ago, my oldest brother, Josh, found himself rather low on funds. He had lost his job earlier in the year, and, unable to find another position in his area of expertise, he had burned through much of his savings. Unwilling to skip gift-giving, he approached my mom with an idea. What if he could bake something?

Josh is a computer genius. He can diagnose any tech problem in seconds. He can build you a custom computer with ease. But his idea of gourmet cooking is simmering a couple of hot dogs on the stovetop before smothering them in ketchup. Mom was skeptical, but Josh insisted. He wanted to give us gifts, and he could afford to buy ingredients. Could she help him? Of course.

What started as a one-time idea became a cherished tradition. First, it was cookie mixes artfully layered in Mason jars. At one point, Josh landed on a chocolate-covered toffee recipe that became a perennial favorite. By the time his financial situation improved, we couldn't imagine Christmas morning without his homemade goodies. Forget the gift cards—bring on the treats!

Then last year, he decided he was ready for a bit more of a challenge. He was gainfully employed at an excellent company that valued him and his work. And he was in love—for the first time, Josh was bringing someone home for Christmas. He felt like a new man, and his tradition needed some updating.

Hunting through family recipes with Mom in early December, he found a stained, faded recipe card immodestly proclaiming "Best Peanut Brittle" in our grandmother's elegant script. "This one," he announced. Mom raised her eyebrows. "That's a little harder than toffee," she cautioned. But again, Josh insisted. So they hauled out the marble slab and set to work.

Christmas morning, when we opened our cookie tins from Josh, the living room filled with cheers. "Yes!" my husband cried, "I love peanut brittle!" "Is this Gram's recipe?" my brother Doug asked. Josh nodded, beaming.

As we munched on candy the rest of the morning, I imagined being back in my grandmother's kitchen. I remembered the heat of the stove and the smell of boiling sugar, and I could almost hear Gram warning me to let it cool just a little longer before sneaking a taste. Legacy is a big word to attach to something like peanut brittle, but in that moment it felt appropriate. Gram seemed to join us and bless our expanding family as we all

enjoyed her beloved recipe. That recipe card was right. It truly is the best peanut brittle.

Gram's Best Peanut Brittle

1 tablespoon butter

2 tablespoons flour

3 cups plus 2 tablespoons granulated sugar, divided

2 cups plus 2 tablespoons natural creamy peanut butter (with oil separation)

1 cup light corn syrup

3 cups raw Spanish peanuts (with skins)

2 teaspoons vanilla extract

¾ teaspoon salt

1 rounded teaspoon baking soda

Coat marble slab with a thin film of butter; sprinkle lightly with flour and 2 tablespoons sugar. Also lightly coat heavy cotton canvas work gloves with butter.

Stir peanut butter to incorporate oil before measuring; pour onto middle of slab.

In a large saucepan, combine remaining 3 cups sugar, corn syrup, and 1 cup water; bring to a boil. Cover and boil 2½ minutes. Add 3 cups peanuts to syrup and boil, stirring constantly, until candy thermometer reaches 300°F. Remove from heat and add vanilla, salt, and baking

soda. Stir quickly to combine; pour hot syrup over peanut butter on slab. As you pour, your friend will use wooden spatulas to quickly blend peanut butter and hot syrup together.

With gloved hands, work together to spread and flatten mixture on slab until it is about ½ inch thick. Cool completely. Break into pieces and store in airtight containers. Makes 8 to 10 servings.

Christmas

Constance Quimby Mills

The frost's on the window;
the wreath's on the door.
The Christmas tree's glittering
from ceiling to floor.

The candlelight flickers;
the firelight glows.
Stockings are hung neatly
all in a row.

The old folks, the young folks
gather together,
from faraway places,
in all types of weather,

to celebrate Christmas
and sing the refrain,
"Glory to God,
peace on earth to all men."

Single Star

Eileen Spinelli

My list of
Christmas tasks
is long.
Candy . . . cards . . .
yards of ribbon.
I tussle with packages
at the car, and then
a single star
brightens,
snagging my
scattered heart.

Is this what
three kings
felt amid their
ancient duties and
decrees—
that something
wondrous was
about to happen
forever?

Best Christmas Morning

Clara Brummert

I remember my sixth Christmas as if it were yesterday. Our neighborhood got a delightful barrage of snow on Christmas Eve, and everyone was caught up in the beauty and good cheer of the season. A foot of fresh snow beneath the dimming afternoon sky kindled the childhood spirit in young and old alike.

Folks bundled up and went out to visit one another. Men gathered with hands in their pockets and caught up on the news while their wives clustered nearby discussing holiday recipes. Teens shoveled driveways while young children rolled balls for lopsided snowmen, and twin girls giggled as they created a collection of angels deep in the drifts.

Up and down the street, Christmas lights glowed through heavy clumps of white on the shrubs. The street looked like a cheerful collection of gingerbread houses with thick frosting on rooftops and bright candy foliage all around.

I used a twig as a baton and marched through the snow, leading a band that consisted of my little brother. After every few steps, the deep snow overcame him, so I ran back to help him up and we marched forward again.

We paraded by Momma as she chatted with a neighbor, and I heard the lady wonder if Daddy was home. Momma explained that we didn't know when he'd get his next leave, and she seemed to grow a little taller when she told the lady how proud Daddy was to serve our country. I was proud too.

As darkness fell, Momma led our little parade back home. Christmas Eve supper was ham on homemade rolls, and we carefully sipped milk from crystal glasses. After we were bathed and zipped into our footed pajamas, we knelt to pray, then crawled into bed.

I listened for Santa's boots to shuffle through the deep snow on the roof, but my eyes grew heavy. Soon, the rich darkness overcame my childhood determination, and I gave in to sleep.

A scraping noise downstairs startled me awake. Jarred from deep sleep, I snuggled deeper under my quilt and stared into the blackness, barely breathing. After a few moments I heard a muffled thump, then a faint clink.

Someone was down there.

I took a few moments to roll my courage and excitement into action, then I slid out of bed.

The soft, warm glow of the tree lights led me down the stairs. There was still no sign of anyone, so I eased across the room.

On the end table, the plate of cookies was empty except for a few crumbs. The milk had been drained from the tall glass, and the carrots were gone from the saucer too.

Toys and gifts bulged beneath the tree. Right out front was the doll from my list.

My eyes scanned the room farther out, searching. And then I saw it.

A bulky knapsack, worn and dusty from travel to faraway lands, rested on the tile. Big boots stood near a heavy coat draped over a chair.

I scanned the living room again and peeked into the kitchen, but no one was there.

I hurried back up the stairs, a bit disappointed, when the last squeaky step let out a loud creak.

Suddenly, Momma's door swung open. Daddy filled the doorway. I froze for a moment, then he was there at the top of the landing, swooping me high into his arms.

"Merry Christmas, sugarplum," he whispered in a hoarse voice. My own voice was lost to the lump in my throat, so I buried my face in his neck and hugged his scratchy chin tighter to my damp cheek.

"Did Thanta come yet?" my little brother lisped groggily, as he appeared in the hall.

Then he rubbed his eyes, gasped, and barreled toward Daddy's other open arm. It was a Christmas gift none of us will ever forget.

Going Home

Joy Belle Burgess

Just down another little road,
and over one more hill,
just through a little quiet town
and then our hearts will thrill—
at being home!

It's just a few more minutes now;
no more we'll be away.
We'll look upon the old home place
and this will be the day—
that we'll be home!

At last we see the snowbound fields,
the old familiar barn,
and there I see the lighted window
glowing with its charm—
guiding us home!

There at the open door we see
the dearest folks on earth;
we'll smile and cry with happiness,
warm like the fire's hearth.
At last we're home!

Let the church bells in the
      valley ring
for all on Christmas Day,
pealing forth with joy for all;
we'll bow our heads to pray.
With thanks, we're home!

We'll have a sumptuous dinner here,
with friends to say "Hello!"
And love will fill each joyous hour,
so deep within, we'll know:
We're home!

Through My Window

Sitting on the Sidelines

Pamela Kennedy

On the afternoon of December 23, last year, we had just finished wrapping up our holiday preparations at the beach cottage where we would celebrate Christmas with our extended family a week later. Our adult children would be spending the twenty-fifth with their in-laws or at their own homes. Then we'd all gather on New Year's Eve to celebrate together. The packages were under the tree, the Christmas bread baked and in the freezer. There was time to return to our city home where we'd enjoy a quiet Christmas Day together before diving into the delightful holiday chaos of eight adults and three young grandchildren.

I was heating up our dinner when my husband came in from outside. He looked a little pale. "I kind of fell," he said, limping over to the counter and leaning against it. His elbow was scraped, but it didn't look too bad. Then he told me what had happened. While carrying some equipment down the concrete steps from our thirteen-foot-high bulkhead to the beach below, his shoes slipped on the slimy stairs and he landed hard on his back and rear end. He was shaken up and bruised, but he hadn't hit his head or broken anything, as far as we could tell. And he didn't want to go to the doctor. So we didn't.

It was a painful night. In the morning, he limped to the car and gingerly hoisted himself into the passenger seat. He reluctantly agreed to stop by the urgent-care clinic on the way home. While the doctor confirmed that there didn't appear to be any permanent damage, he warned us that recovery would take a few weeks at least.

Within a few days, my husband was purple from his waist to his knees. Acute pain prevented him from sleeping or sitting comfortably, and slowly pacing around our condo or leaning against a counter provided only minor relief. It became clear that this Christmas celebration would be quite different from years past.

When we told our sons and daughter about their dad's situation, they were all concerned and immediately leapt into action. Our son-in-law declared that this Christmas, Dad would be promoted to Supervisor. Everyone would pitch in to accomplish the myriad tasks he normally accomplished. He could give direction, but was to "observe and advise" from a distance—preferably in a soft chair.

I was skeptical of how this would work out, but I needn't have worried. Older son, Josh, took care of Papa duties with the grandkids, such as playing piggy-back, doing puzzles, building block structures,

and supervising the plastic racetrack. Younger son, Doug, assumed his father's role of slicing, toasting, buttering, and serving the traditional Julekake for our Christmas breakfast. Daughter, Anne, played elf, stuffing surprises into Christmas stockings and handing out gifts assisted by her five-year-old nephew. Son-in-law, Kevin, carved the "roast beast" under my husband's supervision, and the whole family pitched in with clean-up duties.

When the festivities were over and everyone had left, my husband and I sat in front of a blazing fire that had been set by our son and grandson. He shifted on the couch, trying to find a comfortable position.

"What a great Christmas," I sighed. "I mean except for your being hurt, of course." He chuck-led and said, "It's funny how we assume we're the only ones who can do the things we do. But maybe there's a bit of pride wrapped up in all of that." He smiled wryly. "And just a little bit of control."

I smiled and snuggled closer. "I think everyone really enjoyed helping out and taking on more responsibilities—things they wouldn't have done if you were perfectly healthy," I mused. "It was a special gift to see our family's love from a different perspective."

"Yeah." He was quiet for a moment and then added, "I'm not saying I'd ever want to take another fall, but I have to admit, there are some things you only see once you're stuck on the sidelines."

A Christmas Verse

Eugene Field

Why do the bells of Christmas ring?
Why do little children sing?

Once a lovely shining star,
seen by shepherds from afar,
gently moved until its light
made a manger's cradle bright.

There a darling Baby lay,
pillowed soft upon the hay.
And His mother sang and smiled:
"This is Christ, the holy Child!"

Therefore bells for Christmas ring;
therefore little children sing.

When Christmas Bells Are Ringing

Mrs. W. Baggott

When Christmas bells are ringing
and Christmas carols sung,
when holly and the mistletoe
from door and pane are hung,

when Christmas gifts are
   piled high
beneath the Christmas tree,
you feel content and happy
at the good things that you see.

When Christmas bells are ringing
the carols old and true,
of you, dear friend, I'm thinking.
I send my wish to you.

Right from my heart it travels
through the silent night—
upward, ever upward,
to God's great throne of light.

Then from heaven my wish
   comes stealing
into your heart again,
and you hear the angels' message—
peace, goodwill to men.

When Christmas bells are ringing,
this is the prayer I send,
with old-time Christmas greetings—
God's peace be yours, my friend.

The Quechee Community Church in Quechee, Vermont. Image © James Kirkikis/Shutterstock.

Sing Gloria

Susan Sundwall

Sing Gloria! Sing Gloria!
with angels from on high,
who came in brilliant legions
to light the midnight sky.

Frightened shepherds heard
the hymn

that echoed through the earth:
"Tonight, a Savior has
been born,
we come to hail His birth."

The chosen few, those shepherds,
then hastened on their way,

and found the Baby lying
on a bed of fragrant hay.

Still this story stirs us,
we remember what was done.
Sing Gloria to Jesus,
the Lamb, God's only Son.

Image © Becky Swora/Alamy Stock Photo

*But peaceful was the night
wherein the Prince of light
His reign of peace
upon the earth began.*

—John Milton

What Shall I Give Him?

Christina G. Rossetti

What can I give Him,
poor as I am?
If I were a shepherd
I would bring a lamb;

if I were a Wise Man
I would do my part;
yet what I can I give Him:
give my heart.

The Story of a Song

A Carol for All

Pamela Kennedy

The English lyrics of this Christmas favorite were written in the nineteenth century by James Chadwick, a British bishop. But the angelic chorus, "*Gloria in excelsis Deo*," is much older, first appearing in the gospel of Luke (Luke 2:14). When Pope Telesphorus ordained that "*Gloria in excelsis Deo*" be sung or chanted by first-century monks at a special mass on midnight each Christmas Eve, it became the earliest hymn connected with the celebration of Christ's birth. After Emperor Constantine declared Christianity the official religion of the Roman Empire, fourth-century missionaries traveled to Rome's provinces sharing stories from the Bible with the people they encountered. Tales of angels were especially popular, and quickly became favorite subjects in local poetry and song.

The Christmas carol "Angels We Have Heard on High" originated in the form of a French folk song titled, "*Les Anges Dans nos Campagnes*" or "The Angels in Our Countryside." In 1862, Bishop Chadwick discovered the text and loosely translated the verses into English. He then matched his words with the original French melody, but he transcribed the chorus (meant to communicate the message of the angels) in Latin, accompanied by a melody more reminiscent of a chant. By combining a common tune and language of the people with an ancient melody and language of the church, this carol cleverly made a connection between the secular and the sacred. Everywhere this favorite carol is sung today, in whatever language, the chorus is always sung in Latin, thus maintaining Chadwick's original intent of including voices from both earth and heaven.

Several other contrasting elements in the carol emphasize that this "newborn King" came to bridge the gap between the holy and the common. Angelic voices descend from "on high, sweetly singing o'er the plains," and then these celestial messengers are echoed on earth by "mountains in reply." Angels, in all their heavenly splendor and majesty, appear to the least sophisticated of earthly residents—humble shepherds. When the shepherds are directed to offer adoration and homage to "Christ the Lord, our newborn King," they are sent not to an opulent palace in the city of Jerusalem, but to a lowly stable in the small town of Bethlehem. The carol reminds us again and again that Christ bridges differences of all kinds. And even after two millennia, the ancient message of the angels continues to echo to all, young and old, poor and rich, simple and sophisticated: All people are invited to join the heavenly chorus, "*Gloria in excelsis Deo!*"

Angels We Have Heard on High

Lyrics: Adapted from the French by James Chadwick; Music: French Folk Melody

In a Quiet Stable

Lorna Volk

The hills and vales are silent
and the stars are shining bright.
All the world is waiting
on this calm and holy night.
And in a quiet stable
there is wonderment and awe,
for there a newborn Infant lies
asleep upon the straw.

Little Donkey

Richard Murray

Little donkey on her way
with a steady pace,
bearing Mary, great with Child,
full of love and grace.

Little donkey stops to rest
in Bethlehem one night,
and from a stable she can see
the sky is filled with light.

Little donkey eating hay,
she feels the gentle breeze
of shepherds moving past her
and falling to their knees.

Little donkey hears the cry
of sweet Emmanuel;
she looks at her Creator
and knows that all is well.

The Birth of Christ

Alfred, Lord Tennyson

The time draws near the birth of Christ;
the moon is hid—the night is still;
the Christmas bells from hill to hill
answer each other in the mist.

Four voices of four hamlets round,
from far and near, on mead and moor,
swell out and fail, as if a door
were shut between me and the sound.

Each voice four changes on the wind,
that now dilate and now decrease,
peace and goodwill, goodwill and peace,
peace and goodwill to all mankind.

Rise, happy morn! Rise, holy morn!
Draw forth the cheerful day from night.
O Father! Touch the east, and light
the light that shone when hope was born!

How Wonderful

John C. Bonser

How wonderful, as waiting ends,
that men and angels meet as friends
to celebrate the Christ Child's birth,
as starry peace descends to earth
to bathe with light an ancient town
that will forever be renowned!

How wonderful a manger holds
a King, not clad in silks and golds,
but rather wrapped in swaddling clothes
no court's designer ever chose,
and that a stable's rustic walls
supplant some mansion's stately halls!

How wonderful that Wise Men three
should see at once His deity,
while humble shepherds hear on high
joyful hosannas pierce the sky!
More wonderful, in faith's sunrise—
God's love revealed in Mary's eyes!

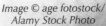
*Image © age fotostock/
Alamy Stock Photo*

Jesus' Birth Foretold

Luke 1:26–27, 30–31, 34–45; 2:1, 3–5

And in the sixth month the angel Gabriel was sent from God unto a city of Galilee, named Nazareth, to a virgin espoused to a man whose name was Joseph, of the house of David; and the virgin's name was Mary.

And the angel said unto her, Fear not, Mary: for thou hast found favour with God. And, behold, thou shalt conceive in thy womb, and bring forth a son, and shalt call his name JESUS.

Then said Mary unto the angel, How shall this be, seeing I know not a man? And the angel answered and said unto her, The Holy Ghost shall come upon thee, and the power of the Highest shall overshadow thee: therefore also that holy thing which shall be born of thee shall be called the Son of God.

And, behold, thy cousin Elisabeth, she hath also conceived a son in her old age: and this is the sixth month with her, who was called barren. For with God nothing shall be impossible. And Mary said, Behold the handmaid of the Lord; be it unto me according to thy word. And the angel departed from her.

And Mary arose in those days, and went into the hill country with haste, into a city of Juda; and entered into the house of Zacharias, and saluted Elisabeth. And it came to pass, that, when Elisabeth heard the salutation of Mary, the babe leaped in her womb; and Elisabeth was filled with the Holy Ghost: And she spake out with a loud voice, and said, Blessed art thou among women, and blessed is the fruit of thy womb. And whence is this to me, that the mother of my Lord should come to me? For, lo, as soon as the voice of thy salutation sounded in mine ears, the babe leaped in my womb for joy. And blessed is she that believed: for there shall be a performance of those things which were told her from the Lord.

And it came to pass in those days, that there went out a decree from Caesar Augustus that all the world should be taxed. And all went to be taxed, every one into his own city. And Joseph also went up from Galilee, out of the city of Nazareth, into Judaea, unto the city of David, which is called Bethlehem; (because he was of the house and lineage of David:) to be taxed with Mary his espoused wife, being great with child.

Jesus Is Born in Bethlehem

Luke 2:6–16; Matthew 2:1–2, 5–11

And so it was, that, while they were there, the days were accomplished that she should be delivered. And she brought forth her firstborn son, and wrapped him in swaddling clothes, and laid him in a manger; because there was no room for them in the inn.

And there were in the same country shepherds abiding in the field, keeping watch over their flock by night. And, lo, the angel of the Lord came upon them, and the glory of the Lord shone round about them: and they were sore afraid. And the angel said unto them, Fear not: for, behold, I bring you good tidings of great joy, which shall be to all people. For unto you is born this day in the city of David a Saviour, which is Christ the Lord. And this shall be a sign unto you; Ye shall find the babe wrapped in swaddling clothes, lying in a manger.

And suddenly there was with the angel a multitude of the heavenly host praising God, and saying, Glory to God in the highest, and on earth peace, good will toward men. And it came to pass, as the angels were gone away from them into heaven, the shepherds said one to another, Let us now go even unto Bethlehem, and see this thing which is come to pass, which the Lord hath made known unto us. And they came with haste, and found Mary, and Joseph, and the babe lying in a manger.

Now when Jesus was born in Bethlehem of Judaea in the days of Herod the king, behold, there came wise men from the east to Jerusalem, saying, Where is he that is born King of the Jews? for we have seen his star in the east, and are come to worship him. And they said unto him, In Bethlehem of Judaea: for thus it is written by the prophet, and thou Bethlehem, in the land of Juda, art not the least among the princes of Juda: for out of thee shall come a Governor, that shall rule my people Israel.

Then Herod, when he had privily called the wise men, enquired of them diligently what time the star appeared. And he sent them to Bethlehem, and said, Go and search diligently for the young child; and when ye have found him, bring me word again, that I may come and worship him also.

When they had heard the king, they departed; and, lo, the star, which they saw in the east, went before them, till it came and stood over where the young child was. When they saw the star, they rejoiced with exceeding great joy. And when they were come into the house, they saw the young child with Mary his mother, and fell down, and worshipped him: and when they had opened their treasures, they presented unto him gifts; gold, and frankincense and myrrh.

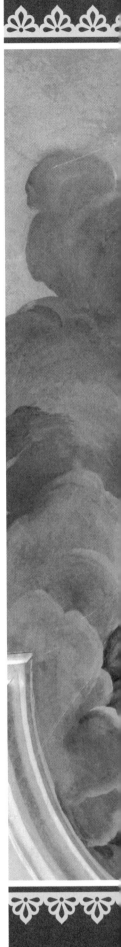

Jesus Is Presented at the Temple

Luke 2:22–38

And when the days of her purification according to the law of Moses were accomplished, they brought [Jesus] to Jerusalem, to present him to the Lord; (As it is written in the law of the LORD, every male that openeth the womb shall be called holy to the LORD;) and to offer a sacrifice according to that which is said in the law of the Lord, A pair of turtledoves, or two young pigeons.

And, behold, there was a man in Jerusalem, whose name was Simeon; and the same man was just and devout, waiting for the consolation of Israel: and the Holy Ghost was upon him. And it was revealed unto him by the Holy Ghost, that he should not see death, before he had seen the Lord's Christ.

And he came by the Spirit into the temple: and when the parents brought in the child Jesus, to do for him after the custom of the law, then took he him up in his arms, and blessed God, and said, Lord, now lettest thou thy servant depart in peace, according to thy word: For mine eyes have seen thy salvation, Which thou hast prepared before the face of all people; A light to lighten the Gentiles, and the glory of thy people Israel. And Joseph and his mother marvelled at those things which were spoken of him.

And Simeon blessed them, and said unto Mary his mother, Behold, this child is set for the fall and rising again of many in Israel; and for a sign which shall be spoken against; (Yea, a sword shall pierce through thy own soul also,) that the thoughts of many hearts may be revealed.

And there was one Anna, a prophetess, the daughter of Phanuel, of the tribe of Aser: she was of a great age, and had lived with an husband seven years from her virginity; and she was a widow of about fourscore and four years, which departed not from the temple, but served God with fastings and prayers night and day. And she coming in that instant gave thanks likewise unto the Lord, and spake of him to all them that looked for redemption in Jerusalem.

PRESENTATION OF JESUS AT THE TEMPLE. *Photograph © Zvonimir Atletic/Shutterstock.*

Good News, Great Joy

Rebecca Barlow Jordan

*But the angel said to them, "Do not be afraid. I bring you good news
that will cause great joy for all the people. Today in the town of
David a Savior has been born to you; he is the Messiah, the Lord."*
Luke 2:10–11 (NIV)

As a minister's daughter, I never knew what to expect when a late-night phone call interrupted our evenings. More often than not, my father would end up in the emergency room or at the home of a church member in crisis. When I married a minister, that pattern only continued in our lives, sometimes even on holidays.

So, when the phone rang on Christmas Eve one year, as it had in times past, I breathed a quick help prayer. But this time the news on the other end of the phone brought a smile with happy anticipation. We had waited eight years for this call—and it was good news of great joy! Our daughter was on her way to the hospital. Our first grandchild was about to be born.

We jumped in our car and stayed just barely within the speed limit, but the trip would last several hours. Would we make it in time? On the way, I thought about the miracle involved in this birth. After so long trying to have a child, our daughter had discovered there was a problem that might need to be corrected with surgery. The very week she was scheduled to visit a specialist, she took one more pregnancy test at home. It had turned out positive!

We arrived with a couple of hours to spare. The halls of the hospital maternity ward were ghostly quiet, with few patients on this festive, holiday evening. After we checked in on our daughter, we moved out into the hallway, joining in-laws to wait for the big moment. Thanks to a good-hearted nurse who chose to look the other way, we stationed ourselves just outside the door, careful to stay out of her way. We paced and we prayed. We swallowed our fears, waited, and then prayed some more.

And then we heard it: a piercing cry just inside the barely cracked-open door. Most would hardly call it angelic, but to us, that loud wail brought heaven's applause, along with tears of joy and a smile to this Mimi's heart. Our first grandbaby had arrived. And a short while later, as I took my turn to coo and gaze into the face of that sweet baby girl, I knew this Christmas Eve was one we would treasure forever—and a story we would repeat to as many as would listen!

Good news begs to be told, not hidden. It longs for an audience to appreciate, to know, to cherish, and to celebrate with the news bearer. I can only imagine the emotions that spilled out that night over two thousand years ago on a hillside near Bethlehem, when the skies filled with brilliant light. The world had waited centuries for this moment. Men had prophesied His coming. And finally, on this night of nights, it was happening.

Faithful shepherds, stumbling over their smelly sheep, bowed to the ground—but not in joy at first. Fear buckled their knees, as their staffs shook with the sound of heaven's host. But then, realizing these angelic beings brought news of great joy, they couldn't leave the hillside fast enough to see for themselves. A babe? Savior of the world? Born in Bethlehem? The good news of great joy spurred them to travel with great haste to the tiny town, where they indeed found Jesus, the promised Babe, lying in a manger.

The same heavenly announcement delivered that star-studded night still beckons us. That good news is for all people (not just grandparents), everywhere, at all times. The good news of Jesus' coming is still the best news we'll ever hear. Great joy for you and me! The Light of the World has come!

A Christmas Carol for Children

Martin Luther

Good news from heaven the angels bring;
glad tidings to the earth they sing:
to us this day a Child is given
to crown us with the joy of heaven.

This is the Christ, our God and Lord,
who in all need shall aid afford.
He will Himself our Savior be,
from sin and sorrow set us free.

To us that blessedness He brings,
which from the Father's bounty springs,
that in the heavenly realm we may
with Him enjoy eternal day.

All hail, Thou noble Guest, this morn,
whose love did not the sinner scorn!

In my distress Thou cam'st to me;
what thanks shall I return to Thee?

Were earth a thousand times as fair,
beset with gold and jewels rare,
she yet were far too poor to be
a narrow cradle, Lord, for Thee.

Ah, dearest Jesus, Holy Child!
Make Thee a bed, soft, undefiled,
within my heart, that it may be
a quiet chamber kept for Thee.

Praise God upon His heavenly throne,
who gave to us His only Son.
For this His hosts, on joyful wing,
a blest New Year of mercy sing.

BABE IN THE MANGER by Simon Mendez. Image © Simon Mendez/Advocate Art.

Christmas Is

Carice Williams

Christmas is for wishing
upon one lovely star;
Christmas is a longing
to be where loved ones are.

Christmas is for dreaming
before the firelight's glow—
dreams of days that are to be
and joys of long ago.

Christmas is for loving
and spreading peace on earth;
Christmas is remembering
our blessed Savior's birth.

It's Christmas

Esther F. Thom

It's Christmas when the pine tree
is trimmed with tinsel bright,
when holly hangs upon the door,
and candles glow at night.

It's Christmas when the table
is graced with Yuletide treats,

the roasted goose, cranberry jam,
plum pudding, nuts, and sweets.

It's Christmas when glad voices sing
in praise to God above,
when peace, goodwill prevail on earth,
and hearts are filled with love.

Image © Masterfile Royalty Free

Light

John C. Bonser

I love the sight of Christmas lights
this season of the year
and merry sounds that now abound
in melodies of cheer!

I love the words that may be heard
in carols that are sung,
the happy cries and sparkling eyes
among the very young!

I love the scenes of evergreens
and wreaths hung everywhere,
soft, falling snow and candleglow
and people bowed in prayer!

I love the bells whose message tells
the sweetest story told—
how goodness still our lives can fill
as God's great plan unfolds!

I love the light, that special night,
the shepherds saw afar
and ran to find for humankind—
His bright and morning star!

This Season

Georgia B. Adams

Midst candleglow and starshine,
midst tree lights all aglow,
we celebrate this season,
the dearest one we know.

We pause for new reflections
upon the Christ Child's birth;
even now the star of Bethlehem
brings hope anew to earth.

And as the snow besilvers
our countryside around,
the angels in the heavens
with tidings glad resound.

We linger at the manger
to capture once again
the awe of that great moment
when God came down to men.

As candleglow and starshine
cast shadows on the wall,
we celebrate this season,
most blessed of them all!

View of Boston, Massachusetts, at Commonwealth Avenue.
Image © Marcio Jose Bastos Silva/Shutterstock.

Take every holiday moment,
hold it close and keep it near.
Make every gleam of candlelight
shine on into next year.
Hear the music of laughter
that brightens all the earth
unite us all for peace
as we celebrate His birth.
—ALBERTA DREDLA

ISBN-13: 978-0-8249-1355-7

Published by Ideals
An imprint of Worthy Publishing Group
A division of Worthy Media, Inc.
Nashville, Tennessee

Copyright © 2018 by Worthy Media, Inc.

Printed and bound in the U.S.A.
Printed on Weyerhauser Lynx. The paper used in this publication meets the minimum requirements of American National Standard for Information Sciences—Permanence of Paper for Printed Materials, ANSI Z39.48-1984.

Publisher, Peggy Schaefer
Editor, Melinda L. R. Rumbaugh
Designer, Marisa Jackson
Associate Editor, Kristi Breeden
Copy Editors, Anne Kennedy Brady, Amanda Sauer

Cover: Image © Sea Wave/Shutterstock
Inside front cover: GOOD OLD DAYS by Nicky Boehme. Image © Nicky Boehme/Art Licensing.
Inside back cover: MERRY CHRISTMAS by Nicky Boehme. Image © Nicky Boehme/Art Licensing.

Sheet Music for "Angels We Have Heard on High" by Dick Torrans, Melode, Inc. Additional art credits: art for "Bits & Pieces," "Family Recipes," back cover spot art, and spot art for pages 1 and 44 by Kathy Rusynyk.

ACKNOWLEDGMENTS

OUR THANKS to the following authors or their heirs: Georgia B. Adams, Mrs. W. Baggott, John C. Bonser, Nora M. Bozeman, Anne Kennedy Brady, Clara Brummert, Joy Belle Burgess, Vincent Godfrey Burns, Lansing Christman, Tracy Crump, Joan Donaldson, Alberta M. Dredla, Patricia Ann Emme, J. Harold Gwynne, Rebecca Barlow Jordan, Polly Prindle Katzenbeger, Pamela Kennedy, Minnie Klemme, LaVerne P. Larson, Pamela Love, Constance Quimby Mills, Richard Murray, Bob Rowe, Eileen Spinelli, Susan Sundwall, Esther F. Thom, Ruth Underhill, Lorna Volk, Carice Williams, Claire Dutton Williams.
    Scripture quotations, unless otherwise indicated, are taken from King James Version (KJV). Public Domain. Scripture quotations marked (NIV) are taken from the Holy Bible, New International Version®, NIV®. Copyright © 1973, 1978, 1984, 2011 by Biblica, Inc.™ Used by permission of Zondervan. All rights reserved worldwide. www.zondervan.com. The "NIV" and "New International Version" are trademarks registered in the United States Patent and Trademark Office by Biblica, Inc.™ Scripture quotations marked NLT are taken from the Holy Bible, New Living Translation, copyright © 1996, 2004, 2007 by Tyndale House Foundation. Used by permission of Tyndale House Publishers, Inc., Carol Stream, Illinois 60188. All rights reserved.
    Every effort has been made to establish ownership and use of each selection in this book. If contacted, the publisher will be pleased to rectify any inadvertent errors or omissions in subsequent editions.

Join the community of Ideals readers on Facebook at: www.facebook.com/IdealsMagazine

Readers are invited to submit original poetry and prose for possible use in future publications. Please send no more than four typed submissions to: Ideals submissions, Worthy Publishing Group, 6100 Tower Circle, Suite 210, Franklin, Tennessee 37067. Editors cannot guarantee your material will be used, but we will contact you if we do wish to publish.